ZEN

WISDOM

AND OTHER MASTERS

Published by Brolga Publishing Pty Ltd
ABN 46 063 962 443
PO Box 12544, A'Beckett Street, Melbourne,
Victoria, Australia, 8006

bepublished@brolgapublishing.com.au
www.brolgapublishing.com.au

National Library of Australia Cataloguing-in-Publication entry:
Zocchi, Mark.
Zen wisdom and other masters
9781921221798 (pbk.)
Zen Buddhism
294.3927

Printed in China by Everbest Printing Co Ltd.
Cover design by David Khan
Typeset by Imogen Stubbs

ZEN
WISDOM
AND OTHER MASTERS

Compiled & illustrated
by Mark Zocchi

INTRODUCTION

Inspired by the Buddha and the great Zen masters, the intention of this little book is to help awaken the reader's own wisdom mind.

Zen Wisdom is filled with quotes, Haiku (Zen Poems) and Koans (traditional riddles that a master asks a student to inspire the student's awakening).

Zen is a school of Buddhism that arose in China around the 4th century CE but was refined in Japan when a South Indian Buddhist monk named Bodhidharma allegedly brought the "mind only" teaching there and started a lineage.

There is one teaching that is thought to be central to Zen. One day the Buddha was to give a teaching to huge assembly of monks and nuns gathered. The Buddha did not speak but simply held up a flower. The crowd became restless and eager for the Buddha's teaching to begin. But a senior disciple, Kashaya, only smiled. The Buddha said Kashaya had understood the teaching and was to be known from then on as Mahakashyapa.

Mahakashyapa understood the highest wisdom of the Buddha. In that moment of the Buddha holding up the flower a direct mind-to-mind transmission had occurred and this is seen as the beginning of the Zen lineage.

Typically Zen is a direct approach were Haiku, and Koan are used to break conceptual thinking leading to a glimpse of satori or enlightenment.

This direct teaching or wisdom teaching is known as *Zen*, *Chaun* in Chinese and *Dzogchen* in Tibetan.

Any attempt to describe Zen in words will fall short, because they are words and not the experience of Zen. Or as one Zen master said, "The finger pointing to the moon is not the moon." However the blessing of the finger pointing to the moon is that it helps turn our focus in the right direction.

May "Zen Wisdom" help turn your mind to uncover your own wisdom.

Zen in its essence
is the art of seeing
into the nature of ones being,
and it points the way
from bondage to freedom.

D.T. SUZUKI

Although I try to hold
the single thought
Of Buddha's teaching in my heart,
I cannot help but hear the many
cricket's voices calling as well.

ISUMI SHIKIBU

We accept the graceful falling
Of mountain cherry blossoms,
But it is much harder for us
To fall away from our own
Attachment to the world

ZEN

When my house burned down
I gained
An unobstructed view
of the moonlight sky

ZEN
(renunciation / letting go)

Out of clutter,
find simplicity.
From discord,
find harmony.
In the middle of difficulty
lies opportunity.

ALBERT EINSTEIN

With plum blossom scent,
This sudden sun emerges
Along a mountain trail

BASHO

You the butterfly-
I, Chuang Tzu's
dreaming heart.

It is in difficult to keep
a beginners mind.
There are many possibilities
in a beginners mind,
but in the expert few.

SUSKI ROSHI

Zen is simply. That state of
centeredness which is here and now.

ALLAN WATTS

The world?
Moonlit water drops
From the crane's bill

ZEN MASTER DOGEN

I my new robe
This morning-
Someone else.

What delight it is
When I blow away ash,
To watch the crimson
Of the glowing fire
And hear the water boil.

TACHIBANA AKEMI

Sit quietly doing nothing,
Spring comes,
And the grass grows
By itself.

ZEN WISDOM (SAYING)

See the world through your Heart.

MZ

Meditating deeply
Reach the depth of the source.
Branching streams cannot compare
to this source.
Sitting alone in a great silence,
even though the heavens turn
and the earth is upset,
you will not even blink

NYOGEN SENZAKI

There is no place in Buddhism
for using effort.
Just be ordinary and nothing special.
Relieve your bowels, pass water,
Put your clothes on
and eat your food.
Ignorant people will laugh at me,
But wise will understand.

LIN-CHI

Refraining from all evil,
Not clinging to birth and death,
Working with deep compassion
for all sentient beings,
respecting those over you
and pitying those below you,
with out any detesting or desiring,
worrying or lamentation –
This what is called Buddha
Do not Search beyond it.

DOGEN

The resting place for the mind
is the heart

BUDDHIST MONK

Do not seek the truth.
Only cease to cherish options.

ZEN SAYING

If we speak of what is real
Even a speck of dust
or grain of sand is real
Yet nothing is real
Everything is illusory
Like the moon reflected in water
Neither real or unreal
is the infinite void

ZEN POEM,
VIETNEMESE BUDDHIST MONK

Spring rain –
under trees
a crystal stream.

Everything that begins also ends.
Make peace with that and all will
be well.

THE BUDDHA

Zen mind is not Zen mind
That is,
if you are attached to Zen mind,
Then you have a problem,
And your way is very narrow.
Throwing away Zen mind
is correct Zen mind.
Only keeping the question,
What is the best way of helping
other people?

SEUNG SAHN

To be enlightened is to be intimate
with all things

ZEN MASTER DOGEN

One who excels in travelling
Leaves no tracks.
One who excels as a warrior
Does not appear formidable.
One who excels in fighting
Is never aroused by anger.
One who excels in employing others
Humbles him self before them.

ZEN TRADITION

To see a a world in a grain of sand
Heaven in a wild flower.
Hold infinity
in the palm of your hand
And eternity in an hour.

WILLIAM BLAKE

The Zen of doing anything is doing with a particular concentration of mind, a calmness and simplicity of mind that brings the experience of enlightenment and, through that experience happiness.

D T SUZUKI

All that we are is the result
of what we have thought.
It is founded on our thoughts,
It is made up of our thoughts

THE DHAMMAPADA

Now cat's done
mewing, bedroom's
touched by moonlight.

There is nothing good or bad,
but thinking makes it so.

WILLIAM SHAKESPEARE

Sick on a journey—
over parched fields
dreams wander on.

君子之風

Ask not what tomorrow may bring
But count as blessing
Every day that fate allows you.

HORACE

Every Day is a good day.

UNMON

Every thing comes
at its appointed time

I CHING

Do not dwell in the past
Do not dream of the future.
Concentrate the mind
On the present moment.

BUDDHA

If you really know how to live,
what better way to start the day
with a smile?
Smiling helps you approach the day
with gentleness and understanding.
Smile with your whole being.

THICH NHAT HANH

The Universe doesn't make mistakes

CHRIS PRENTISS

Meditating deeply...
Reach the depth of the source.
Branching streams
Cannot compare to this source!
Sitting alone in a great silence,

He who binds to himself a joy
Does the winged life destroy;
But he who kisses joy as it flies
Lives in Eternity sunrise.

WILLIAM BLAKE

Do not forget the,
blooming
in the thicket.

We are here and it is now.
Further Than that all
human knowledge
Is moonshine.

H.L. MENCKEN

Your worst enemy cannot harm you
As much as your own thoughts,
unguarded.
But once mastered,
No one can help you as much.

THE DHAMMAPA

Summer grasses,
all that remains
of soldiers' dreams.

Think with your whole body

TAISEN DESHIMARU

Out of eternity
The new day is born
Into eternity at night will return.

THOMAS CARLYLE

When you arise in the morning
Give thanks for the morning light.
Give thanks for life and strength.
Give thanks for your food.
And give thanks for the joy of
living.
And if perchance you see no reason
to give thanks
Rest assured the fault is yours.

AMERICAN INDIAN SAYING

Even if it is painful and lonely
associate with worthy companions

DOGEN

To see the things of the present moment
Is to see all that is now,
All that has been since time began,
And all that shall be unto the world's end;
For all things are of
One kind and one form

MARCUS AURELIUS

Another haiku?
Yet more cherry blossoms—
not my face.

The sage blends everything into a harmonious whole. He is unmindful of the confusion and the gloom, and equalizes the humble and the honourable.

CHUANG TZU

Everything that happens to us is for our complete benefit.

CHRIS PRENTISS

The only way to make sense out of change is to plunge with it, move with it, and join in the dance.

ALLAN WATTS

Dew-drops-
how better wash away
world's dust?

He who has once known contentment
The contentment that
Comes simply through being content
Will never again be otherwise than
contented.

TOA TE CHING

To find perfect composure in the midst of change is to find nirvana

SHUNRYU SUZUKI

When you can be calm
in the midst of activity,
This is the true state of nature…
When you can be happy
in the midst of hardship,
then you see the true potential of
the mind

HAUCHU DAOREN

If you laugh at misfortune, you will
not be overcome by it.

VALLUVAR

Know all things like this
A mirage, a cloud castle
Nothing appears as it is.

THE BUDDHA

If I'd the knack
I'd sing like
cherry flakes falling.

Dying cricket–
how full of
life, his song.

The university always strikes you at
your weakest point
Because that's what needs most
strengthening

CHRIS PRENTISS

We accept the graceful falling
Of mountain cherry blossoms,
But it is much harder for us
To fall away from our own
Attachment to the world

ZEN

The miracle is not fly in the air or
walk on water,
but to walk on the earth

CHINESE PROVERB

Do not pursue the past
Do not lose your self in the future
The past no longer is.
The future is yet to come.
Looking very deeply at life as it is
here and now;
The practitioner dwells in stability
and freedom

BHADDEKARATTA SUTTA

The present moment is a wonderful moment

THICH NHAT HANH

If the mind is never aroused toward objects,
Then wherever you walk is the site of enlightenment

POA-CHIH

Friends part
forever-wild geese
lost in cloud.

Yellow rose petals
thunder-
a waterfall.

Never say "can not" for you are
infinite
Even time and space are as nothing
compared
With your nature.
You can do anything

SWAMI VIVEKANANDA

Live life Abundantly
This is why you have it.
Don't fear don't contract
Open and enjoy.

MZ

The Birds have vanished into the sky
And now the last cloud fades away.
We sit together, the mountain and I,
Until only the mountain remains

LI PO

To abandon what is harmful,
To adopt what is wholesome,
To purify the heart and mind:
This is the teaching of the Buddha.

BUDDHA

The Only truth you find at the top
of the mountain
Is the truth you brought with you.

ZEN SAYING

If you want to be happy, Be.

TOLSTOY

The gap between what is and what "should be", is an ocean of distress.

CHRISTINA FELDMAN

I have three things to teach;
Simplicity, patience and compassion,
These three are your great treasures,
Simple actions and in thought,
You return to the source of being,
Patience with both friends and
enemies,
You accord with the way things are,
Compassionate toward yourself,
You reconcile all beings in the world.

TAO TE CHING

First winter rain-
I plod on,
Traveller, my name.

Contentment is the great elixir

SOGYAL RINPOCHE

Breathing in, I calm my body,
Breathing out, I smile.
Dwelling in the present moment
I know this a wonderful moment.

THICH NHAT HANH

If you are in the moment,
you are in the infinite.

SVAMI PRAJNANPAD

Of what avail is it if we can travel
to the moon,
If we cannot cross the abyss that
separates us from ourselves,
This is the most important of
all journeys
And without it all of the rest are useless

THOMAS MERTON

While moon sets
atop the trees,
leaves cling to rain.

Within your own house swells the treasure of joy,
So why do you go begging from door to door?

SUFI SAYING

The enlightened person is not
exempt from any form
Of feelings but is not bound or
governed by them.
The arrow will hurt, but the pain of
the body will not be matched by the
sorrow and struggle in the mind.

CHRISTINA FELDMAN

Surrendering the story is not a
dismissal of the wounded leg,
but an empowerment, releasing the
capacity to care for what needs
to be cared for with compassion and
responsiveness, letting go of all the
extra layers of fear, apprehension,
and blame.

CHRISTINA FELDMAN

In the pursuit of knowledge, every day something is gained.
In the pursuit of freedom, everyday something is let go.

TAO

Renunciation is not getting rid of
things of this world,
But accepting that they pass away

AITKEN ROSHI

Practicing meditation is to be aware, to smile, to breathe.

THICH NHAT HANH

When you walk, just walk. When you sit, just sit. Just be your ordinary natural self in ordinary life, unconcerned in seeking for Buddhahood. When you're tired, lie down. The fool will laugh at you but the wise man will understand.

LIN CHI

How I long to see
among dawn flowers,
the face of God.

What is this moment lacking?

ZEN QUESTION

No one who truly loves themselves
would harm another,
For they would be harming themselves.

BUDDHA

Everyone sooner or later,
Sits down to a basket of consequences

ROBERT LOUIS STEVENSON

Long accustomed to contemplating
compassion,
I no longer see a difference between
myself and other.

MILAREPA

Better than a thousand careless words
is one single word that gives peace.
Better than a hundred years lived
heedlessness,
Without contemplation,
Is on single day lived in wisdom
and deep contemplation.
Better than a hundred years lived
in confusion,
Is a single day lived with courage
and wise intention.

THE DHAMMAPADA

Nothing can do us more harm than
a thought unguarded
But once understood there is nothing
that can be a greater friend,
Not even your father and mother.

BUDDHA

The universe is change, our life is what our thoughts make it.

MARCUS AURELIUS

Poor boy-leaves
moon-viewing
for rice-grinding.

Earth brings us to life and
nourishes us.
Earth takes us back again.
Birth and death are present in
every moment.

THICH NHAT HANH

Death is extraordinary like life,
when we know how to live.
You cannot live without dying.
You cannot live if you do not die
psychologically every minute.

KRISHNAMURTI

When we begin to practice the basic meditation of tranquillity meditation [shamatha], we may find that our mind won't stay still for a moment. But this condition is not permanent and will change as we practice. Eventually we will be able to place our mind at rest at will, at which point we will have successfully alleviated the manifest disturbance of the disturbing emotions. After developing tranquillity meditation, we can

then apply the second technique,
of insight meditation [vipashyana],
which consists of learning to
recognise and directly experience
the nature of our own mind. This
nature is referred to as emptiness.
When we recognise this nature, and
rest in it, then all of the disturbing
emotions that arise dissolve into
this emptiness and are no longer
afflictions. This is the freedom,
which is called Buddhahood.

KHENCHEN THRANGU RINPOCHE

I'd rather be happy than right.

RAM DASS

Out behind the ideas of
wrongdoing and right doing
There is a field, I'll meet you there,
When the soul lies down in
that grass,
The world is too full to talk about
Ideas, language, even the phrase
"each other"
Does not make sense

SUFI RUMI

If you want to know what compassion is,
Look into the eyes of a mother as
She cradles her fevered, ill child.

BUDDHA

We can not always fix every
event distress,
But can always be present, awake,
and receive each moment with
compassion and simplicity.

CHRISTINA FELDMAN

The only lasting beauty is beauty is
beauty of the heart.

SUFI RUMI

I am unable to restrain external
things, but I shall restrain my
own mind. What need is there to
restrain anything else?

SHANTIDEVA

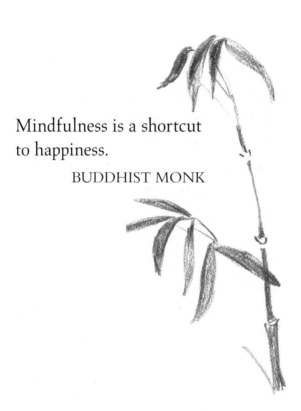

Mindfulness is a shortcut
to happiness.

BUDDHIST MONK

Enlightenment is like the
moon reflected on the water,
The moon does not get wet,
nor is the water broken.
Although its light is wide and great
The moon is reflected even by
a puddle an inch wide,
The whole moon and the entire sky
are reflected in one dew drop on
the grass.

DOGEN

The Real voyage of discovery lies
not in finding new landscapes,
But in having new eyes.

MARCEL PROUST

In this moment what is lacking.

ZEN SAYING

Learn to be happy, here and now, under all conditions; and to include others' happiness in your own joy. Go out of your way to make others happy.

PARAMAHANSA YOGANANDA

Bright moon: I
stroll around the pond—
hey, dawn has come.

Learning to meditate is the greatest gift you can give yourself in this life.

SOGYAL RINPOCHE

If the inner mind has been tamed,
the outer enemy cannot harm you.

ATISA

What life can compare with this?
Sitting quietly by the window, I
watch leaves fall and the flowers
bloom as the seasons come and go.

SECCHO

Not thinking about anything is Zen. Once you know this, walking, standing, sitting or lying down, everything you do is Zen.
To know that the mind is empty is to see the Buddha. Using the mind to look for reality is delusion. Not using the mind to look for reality is awareness. Freeing yourself from words is liberation.

BODHIDHARMA

Such fragrance-
from where.
which tree?

Act without acting on.
Work without working at.

LAO TZU

When sitting, sit; when standing, stand. Above all, don't wobble.

ZEN SAYING

The fundamental delusion of
humanity is to suppose that I
am here and you are out there.

YASUTANI ROSHI

We are what we think.
All that we are arises with
our thoughts.
With our thoughts we make
the world.
Speak or act with an impure mind
and trouble will follow you.
As the wheel follows the ox that
draws the cart.
We are what we think.
All that we are arises with our
thoughts. With our thoughts we
made the world.
Speak or act with a pure mind
and happiness will follow you
As your shadow unshakeable.

THE DHAMMAPADA

…To see the world in a grain of sand,
And a heaven in a wild flower,
Hold infinity in the palm of your hand
And eternity in an hour.

WILLIAM BLAKE

Spring-through
morning mist,
what mountain's there?

When my house burned down
I gained
An unobstructed view of
the moonlit sky

ZEN

To a sincere student,
Every day is a fortunate day

SUZUKI ROSHI

The foolish reject what they see;
The wise reject what they think.

ZEN SAYING

Obey the nature of things and you
will walk freely and undisturbed

SENG-TS'AN

The truth is always near at hand,
within your reach.

D.T. SUZUKI

The who world is a door of
liberation, inviting us to enter.

ZEN SAYING

Write in your heart
That every day
Is the best day of the year

RALPH WALDO EMERSON

The highest nobility lies in taming
your own mind

ATHISA

Come, see real
flowers
of this painful world.

Take time to listen to what
is not said without words
To obey the law too subtle
to be written
To worship the unnameable,
And to embrace the unformed

LAO TUZ

To breath out, let go of the story,
And find the generosity to be
wholeheartedly present

CHRISTINA FELDMAN

There are no ordinary moments.

DAN MILLMAN

As soon as you have made a
thought, laugh at it.

LAO TZU

It is easier to go up the hill than down,
But the view is from the top.

ARNOLD BENNETT

From the withered tree
the flower blooms.

SHOYO ROKO

This zendo is not a peaceful haven
but a furnace room for combustion
of our egotistical delusions.

EIDO ROSHI

To be uncertain is to be uncomfortable, but to be certain is to be ridiculous.

CHINESE WISDOM

The three great vices seem to be efficiency, punctuality, and the desire for achievement and success. They are the things that make people so unhappy and so nervous.

LIN YUTANG

By letting it go it gets all done.
The world is won by those who let
it go. But when you try and try,
the world is beyond the winning.

LAO TZU

Grant yourself a moment of peace and you will understand how foolishly you have scurried about. Learn to be silent and you will notice that you have talked too much.

TSCHEN TSCHI JU

Besides the noble art of getting things done, there is a nobler art of leaving things undone. The wisdom of life consists in the elimination of nonessentials.

LIN YUTANG

All beings are on the path,
all victims of the same existence.
No one is better than the next person.

DENG MING-DAO

The best person is like water.
Water is good; it benefits all
things and does not compete
with them. It dwells in lowly
places that all disdain.

FROM THE TAO TE CHING

The softest things in the world
overcome the hardest things
in the world.

LAO TZU

The best soldier does not attack.
The superior fighter succeeds
without violence. The greatest
conqueror wins without struggle.
The most successful manager leads
without dictating.

FROM THE TAO TE CHING

If you realize that you have enough, you are truly rich.

FROM THE TAO TE CHING

He who grasps loses.

LAO TZU

So if loss of what gives
happiness causes you
distress when it fades, you
can now understand that
such happiness is worthless.

CHUANG TZU

Summer grasses,
all that remains of soldiers' dreams.

BASHO

When anger rises,
think of the consequences.

CONFUCIUS

If you are patient in one moment of anger, you will escape a hundred days of sorrow.

CHINESE PROVERB

Life is a series of natural
and spontaneous changes.
Don't resist them – that only
creates sorrow. Let reality be
reality. Let things flow naturally
forward in whatever way they will.

FROM THE TAO TE CHING

What the caterpillar calls the end,
the rest of the world calls a butterfly.

LAO TZU

A tree that is unbending
is easily broken.

LAO TZU

To be the best person be careful of these things: Your face that it may always reflect kindness; your manners that they might show respect for other people; your words that they may be true; your dealings with other people that they may be fair.

CONFUCIUS

Kindness in words creates confidence. Kindness in thinking creates profoundness. Kindness in giving creates love.

LAO TZU

Fragrance always clings to the hand
that gives you roses.

CHINESE PROVERB

Manifest plainness, embrace
simplicity, reduce selfishness,
have few desires.

LAO TZU

He who knows he has
enough is rich.

FROM THE TAO TE CHING

Silence is a source of great strength.

LAO TZU

Music in the soul can be heard by
the universe.

LAO TZU

To have peace in ones' soul is the
greatest happiness.

ORIENTAL WISDOM

Whenever you hear that someone else has been successful, rejoice. Always practice rejoicing for others – whether your friend or your enemy. If you cannot practice rejoicing, no matter how long you live, you will not be happy.

LAO TZU

Buddha's death-day-
old hands
clicking rosaries.

What life can compare to this?
Sitting quietly by the window, I
watch the leaves fall and the flowers
bloom, as the seasons' come and go.

HSUEH TOU

We sat together, the forest and I,
merging into silence. Until only the
forest remained.

LI PO

Drinking tea, eating rice, I pass
my time as it comes; looking down
at the stream, looking up at the
mountain, how serene and relaxed I
feel indeed!

ZEN POEM

To the mind that is still, the whole universe surrenders.

LAO TZU

We reflect on paradox: water wears away rock. Spirit overcomes force. The weak will undo the mighty. May we learn to see things backwards, inside out, and upside down.

LAO TZU

Contemplating the clear moon
Reflecting a mind empty
as an open sky
Drawn by beauty,
I lose myself
In the shadows it casts.

DOGEN

The only way
To make sense out of change
Is to plunge with it
Move with it,
And join the dance.

ALLAN WATTS

Outside teaching;
part from tradition.
Not founded on words and letters.
Pointing directly
to the human mind.
Seeing into one's nature
and attaining.

BUDDHAHOOD

When I begin to sit
With the dawn in solitude,
I begin to really live.
It makes me treasure
Every single moment of life

GLORIA VANDERBILT

If you cant find the truth
right where you are,
where else do you expect to find it?

DOGEN

Seeing through to essential nature is
the window of enlightenment.

HAKUUN YASUTANI ROSHI

Those with limited views
Are fearful and irresolute;
The faster the hurry,
The slower they go.

SENG-TS'AN

To those who have conformed
Themselves to the Way,
The Way readily
Lends its power

TAO TE CHING

We can ourselves leaning in to the
future that has not arrived,
Or leaning back into the past that
has long gone
This is the very moment that we
can calmly stand in the moment
Letting go of our resistance on the
breath and soften our warm hearts

MZ

One who does not grasp hold of
anything is not agitated.
One who is not agitated is close
to freedom.

BUDDHA

Every time you smile at someone,
it is an action of love, a gift to that
person, a beautiful thing.

MOTHER THERESA

Stop talking and thinking, then
there is nowhere you cannot go.
Returning to the source, you gain
the meaning; chasing forms, you
lose the wholeness. A moment's true
insight transcends all.

SOSAN

My mind is the guiding-reign

THE BUDDHA

Old pond,
leap-splash-
a frog.

When my heart is at peace,
the world is at peace.

CHINESE PROVERB

When I let go of what I am,
I become what I might be.

LAO TZU

Loneliness –
caged cricket dangling
from the wall.

Fidelity to grace in my life is fidelity to simplicity, rejecting ambition and analysis and elaborate thought, or even elaborate concern. A breath of Zen blows all these cobwebs out the window.

THOMAS MERTON

Upon goodness of heart is
built wise attention;
Upon wise attention is
built liberating wisdom

BUDDHA

The definition of an enlightened
person is that they always have
what they need.
Whether sitting alone on a
mountain,
Or in the middle of a crowd,
There is no sense of anything
absent or lacking.

BAKER ROSHI

Out of clutter,
find simplicity.
From discord,
find harmony.
In the middle of difficulty
lies opportunity.

ALBERT EINSTEIN

Chilling autumn rains
Curtain Mount Fuji, then make it
More beautiful to see

BASHO

Flow with whatever may happen
and let your mind be free:
Stay centred by accepting whatever
you are going. This is the ultimate.

CHUANG TZU

South Valley-
wind brings
a sent of snow.

As yesterday is history
And tomorrow may never come,
I have resolved from this day on,
I will do the business I can honestly,
have all the good I can do willingly,
and save my digestion by thinking
pleasantly.

ROBERT LOUIS STEVENSON

Tomb, bend
to autumn wind—
my sobbing.

The true man sees what the eye sees,
and does not add to some thing that
is not there.
He hears what the ears hear
and does not detect imaginary
undertones or overtones. He is
not busy with hidden meaning.

CHUNG TZU

The quieter you become
The more you are able to hear.

ZEN SAYING

Zen
Is not some kind of excitement,
But merely concentration
On our usual every day life.

                SHRUNKYU SUZUKI

Silence is a friend
That will never betray

CONFUCIUS

We are not in chaos
we are the chaos.

MZ

Calming,
Smiling,
Present moment,
Wonderful moment.

THICH NHAT HANH

You must be the change you
wish to see in the world.

MAHATMA GANDHI

Loving what is

BYRON KATIE

The only true strength is a strength that people do not fear.

LAO TZU

When you're deluded, every statement is an ulcer; when you're enlightened, every word is wisdom.

ZHIQU

No thought, no reflection, no analysis, no cultivation, no intention; let it settle itself.

YING-AN

Form is empty of a separate
self, but it is full of everything
else in the cosmos. The same is
true with feelings, perceptions,
mental formations, and
consciousness.

THICH NAT HANH

As we do consistent, patient zazen we begin to know that we are nothing but attachments; they rule our lives. But we never lose an attachment by saying it has to go. Only as we gain true awareness of its true nature does it quietly and imperceptibly wither away; like a sandcastle with waves rolling over, it just smoothes out and finally Where is it? What was it?

CHARLOTTE JOKO BECK

No matter how many years you sit doing zazen, you will never become anything special.

ZEN MASTER SAWAKI

Let your mind wander in
simplicity, blend your spirit
with the vastness, follow along
with things the way they are,
and make no room for personal
views – then the world will
be governed.

CHUANG-TZU

God has no religion.

MAHATMA GANDHI

All conditioned things are impermanent. Work out your own salvation with diligence.

THE BUDDHA'S LAST WORDS

Do not mistake understanding for realisation, and do not mistaken realisation for liberation.

TIBETAN SAYING

Giving is the first of the six perfections. Mind is beyond measure. Things are given beyond measure. Moreover, in giving, mind transforms the gift and the gift transforms mind.

ZEN MASTER DOGEN

Day after day the sun.

ZEN SAYING

He who wherever he goes is attached to no person and to no place by ties of flesh; who accepts good and evil alike, neither welcoming the one nor shrinking from the other – take it that such a one has attained Perfection.

BHAGAVAD-GITA

Do not speak – unless it
improves on silence.

BUDDHIST SAYING

The journey of a thousand miles
must begin with a single step.

LAO TZU

If you understand, things are just as they are; if you do not understand, things are just as they are.

ZEN PROVERB

Your Treasure House is in
yourself, it contains all you need.

HUI HAI

When the pupil is ready to learn, a teacher will appear.

ZEN PROVERB

Teachers open the door…
Your enter by yourself.

CHINESE PROVERB

Before enlightenment:
chop wood, carry water.
After enlightenment:
chop wood, carry water.

OLD ZEN SAYING

We cannot see our reflection in running water. It is only in still water that we can see.

TAOIST PROVERB

The world is like a mirror. Smile and your friends smile back.

JAPANESE ZEN SAYING

A flower falls even though we love it and a week grows even though we do not love it.

DOGEN ZENJI

No road to happiness or
sorrow… Find them in yourself.

CHINESE PROVERB

When is the path? The Zen
Master Nan-sen was asked.
Everyday life is the path,
he answered.

MASTER NAN-SEN

If you light a lamp for
somebody, it will also
brighten your own path.

BUDDHIST SAYING

We are shaped by our thoughts;
we become what we think. When
the mind is pure, joy follows like
a shadow that never leaves.

BUDDHA

It takes a wise man to learn from
his mistakes, but an even wiser
man to learn from others.

ZEN PROVERB

Not thinking of good, not thinking of evil – tell me, what was your original face before your mother and father were born?

ZEN KOAN

In Zen there is nothing to explain,
Nothing to teach that will add to
your knowledge.
Unless it grows out of yourself, no
knowledge is really of value to you a
borrowed plumage never grows.

D T SUZUKI

Zen is expressed simply by sitting

SHUNRYU SUZUKI ROSHI

Living beings are numberless,
I vow to save them all
Confusions are inexhaustible,
I vow to cut them all
Dharma gates are boundless,
I vow to enter them all,
The Buddha-way is unattainable,
I vow to attain it.

BODHISATTVA VOW

The supreme good is like water,
Which nourishes all things
without trying to.

LAO TZU

You should practice like your head is on fire.

OLD ZEN SAYING

Softness triumphs over hardness
What is more malleable is
always superior over that
which immovable

LAO TZU

Anything on the path can
be used for realisation.

LO JONG TEACHINGS
(TIEBETAN TERM)

Try not localize the mind
anywhere, but let it fill up the
whole body, let flow through out
the totality of your being.
When this happens you use your
hands where they are needed , you
use your legs and eyes where they
are needed and no time or energy
to waste.

TAKUAN SOHO (ADVICE TO A
YOUNG SAMURAI)

"The ear hears sounds but the mind does not move"

HUI-NENG
(ON THE ENLIGHTENED MIND).

Mother I knew
Every time I see the ocean
Every time

BASHO
17TH CENTURY ZEN MONK
(HAIKU)

The religion is real living;
living with all ones soul,
with all ones goodness.

ALBERT EINSTEIN

I think of all the places I've been,
Chasing from one famous spot
to another,
Who would guess I'd end up
under a pine tree,
Clasping my knees in the
whispering cold?

HAN-SHAN

Illusory dreams, phantom flowers –
Sixty seven years
A white bird vanishes in the moist,
Autumn waters merge with the sky.

HUNG-CHIH ZEN MASTER

Elements of the Self,
come and go like clouds
with out purpose.

ZEN SAYING

If you can rid your self of
conceptual thought, you
will have accomplished
everything.

HUANG PO

Trust in things being as
they are is the secret of life.

JOKO BECK

Zen is not some fancy,
special art of living,
Our teaching is just to
live, always in reality,
In its exact sense.

SHUNRYU SUZUKI

Life is the way it is.

JOKO BECK

Be a lamp unto yourself

THE BUDDHA

Theresa task to do , and we just need to do it, fear or no fear. I struggle with my life because instead of just doing what needs to needs to be done, I fight the under lying fear.

JOKO BECK

Anything on the path can be used

Fear is an illusion

JOKO BECK

In walking just walk.
In sitting, just sit.
Above all, don't wobble.

YUN – MEN

As a man thinketh in his heart,
so is he.

PROVERBS 23:7

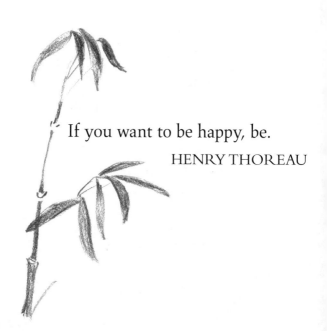

If you want to be happy, be.

HENRY THOREAU

The Tao is near and people
seek it faraway.

MENCIUS

I am not ashamed to
confess that I am ignorant
of what I do not know.

CICERO

A man with outward
courage dares to die
A man with inward
courage dares to live.

LAO-TZU

There's nothing in the world
so admired as a man
Who knows how to bear
unhappiness with courage.

SENECA

Fear always springs from ignorance.

RALPH WALDO EMMERSON

Life is either a daring
adventure or nothing.

HELEN KELLER

The universe is change;
our life is what our
thoughts make it.

MARCUS AURELIUS

We are what we think.
All that we are arises
with our thoughts.
With our thoughts
we make the word.

THE BUDDHA

Unhappy with your life,
change your thinking.

MARK Z

In the World of Reality
there is no self.
There is no other-than-self.

SENFG–T'SAN

Attachment is the greatest fabricator of illusions; reality can be attained only by some one who is detached.

SIMONE WEIL

The words of truth are
always paradoxical.

LAO-TZU

Form is emptiness, and the
very emptiness is form;
Emptiness does not differ
from form, form does not
differ from emptiness;
Whatever is form, that
is emptiness, what ever
emptiness, that is form.

HEART SUTTRA

You must be the change you
wish to see in the world.

MAHATMA GANDHI

To be wronged is nothing
unless you continue to
remember it.

CONFUCIUS

This above all; to thine
own self be true,
And it must follow,
as the night the day,
Thou canst not be false
to any man.

SHAKESPEARE

Oure limited self is the wall separating us from the self of God. It is being to self that is the recognition of God.

HAZART INAYAT KHAN

All life is an experiment.

OLIVER WENDELL HOLMES

Ask and it shall be given unto you.
Seek and it shall be given.

LUKE 11:9

The only lasting beauty is
the beauty of the heart.

RUMI

The Spirit of the Buddha
is that of great loving
kindness and compassion.

BUDDHA

The highest wisdom is
loving kindness.

THE TALMUD

Very little is needed to
make a happy life.
It is all within yourself,
in your way of thinking.

MARCUS AURELIUS

Accustomed long to
contemplating Love
and Compassion,
I forgotten all difference
between myself and others.

MILAREPA

In your own house dwells
the treasure of joy;
So why do you go begging
from door to door?

SUFI SAYING

The discipline man masters
thoughts by stillness
And emotions by calmness.

LAO-TZU

The longer I live the more beautiful life becomes.

FRANK L WRIGHT

Do not seek the truth
stop having an opinion.

SENG-T'SAN

Mankind's role is to fulfil his heaven-sent purpose through a sincere heart that is in harmony with all creation and love all things.

MORIHEI UESHIBA

Everything flows on and
on like this river, without
pause, day and night.

CONFUCIUS.

How can I be still,
By flowing with the stream

LAO TUZ

Underlying great doubt there
is great satori, where there
is thorough questioning
there will be thorough going
experience of awakening.

ZEN SAYING

Awaken the mind without
fixing it anywhere.

DIAMOND SUTRA

Not Knowing how near the truth is,
People seek it far away, what a pity!
They are like him who in the
midst water,
Cries in thirst so imploringly.

HAKIUN

If we walk
The true Way
In our inmost heart
Even without praying
God will be with us!

TAKUAN

If we wish to die well we,
must learn how to live well.

HIS HOLINESS DL

ZEN WISDOM
AND OTHER MASTERS

	Qty
RRP AU$15.99	.....
Postage within Australia AU$5.00	.....

TOTAL★ $_____ ★All prices include GST

Name: ....Phone:................................

Address: ....

Email: ....

Payment: ❏ Money Order ❏ Cheque ❏ Amex ❏ MasterCard ❏ Visa

Cardholder's Name: ....

Credit Card #: __ __ __ __   __ __ __ __   __ __ __ __   __ __ __ __

Signature: ....

Expiry Date: __ __ / __ __

Allow 10 days for delivery.

Payment to: Better Bookshop (ABN 14 067 257 390)
PO Box 12544
A'Beckett Street, Melbourne, 8006
Victoria, Australia
Fax: +61 3 9879 3936
sales@brolgapublishing.com.au

BE PUBLISHED

Publishing through a successful Australian publisher. Brolga provides:

- Editorial appraisal
- Cover design
- Typesetting
- Printing
- Author promotion
- National book trade distribution, including sales, marketing and distribution through Macmillan Australia.

For details and inquiries, contact:
Brolga Publishing Pty Ltd
PO Box 12544
A'Beckett St VIC 8006
ABN: 46 063 962 443

Phone: 03 9600 4982
bepublished@brolgapublishing.com.au
markzocchi@brolgapublishing.com.au